The Taming of the Screw

The Taming of the Screw

Several million homeowners' problems
sidestepped by **Dave Barry**

Illustrated by Jerry O'Brien

 Rodale Press, Emmaus, Pennsylvania

Printed in the United States of America on acid-free paper ∞

Book design by Bill Bosler
Art direction by Karen A. Schell

Library of Congress Cataloging in Publication Data

Barry, Dave.
    The taming of the screw.

    Includes index.
    1. Dwellings—Maintenance and repair—Anecdotes,
facetiae, satire, etc. I. Title.
PN6231.D67B37 1983   643'.7'0207   83-11205
ISBN 0-87857-484-0 paperback

Distributed in the book trade by St. Martin's Press

10   paperback

Contents

DAVE AND MR. SCREWY

Introduction

Sincere statement of thanks from the author

I sincerely thank you for purchasing this do-it-yourself book, instead of one of the thousands of other, much better ones. I want to assure you that there is not a single project in this book that I would not have considered doing myself if I hadn't been so busy writing a do-it-yourself book.

Why you need this book

If you're like most homeowners, you're afraid that many repairs around your home are too difficult to tackle. So when your furnace explodes, you call in a so-called professional to fix it. The "professional" arrives in a truck with lettering on the sides and deposits two assistants whose combined IQ's would still be a two-digit number, and they spend the better part of a week in your basement whacking objects at random with heavy wrenches, after which the "professional" returns and gives you a bill for slightly more money than it would cost you to run a successful campaign for the U.S. Senate.

And that's why you've decided to start doing things yourself. You figure, "If those bozos can fix my furnace, then so can I. How difficult can it be?"

Very difficult. In fact, most home projects are impossible, which is why you should do them yourself. There is no point in paying other people to screw things up when you can easily screw them up yourself for far less money. This book can help you.

How to use this book

The best way to use this book is to place it on a coffee table so that your guests can place their drinks on it. Or, if you'd like to attempt a home repair project, you can look up the appropriate chapter. For example, if you want to fix a plumbing problem, you'd look up Chapter 4, "Plumbing." Or Chapter 8, "Masonry." It won't make much difference.

Chapter 1

Tools

Why they want to injure you, and how to thwart them

Basically, a tool is an object that enables you to take advantage of the laws of physics and mechanics in such a way that you can seriously injure yourself. Today, people tend to take tools for granted. If you're ever walking down the street and you notice some people who look particularly smug, the odds are that they are taking tools for granted. If I were you, I'd walk right up and smack them in the face.

We ought to be very grateful that we have tools. Millions of years ago people did not have them, and home projects were extremely difficult. For example, when a primitive person wanted to put up paneling, he had to drive the little paneling nails into the cave wall with his bare fist, so generally the paneling wound up getting spattered with primitive blood, which isn't really all that bad when you consider how ugly paneling is to begin with.

MANDRILL

OSCREWDRIVERICH

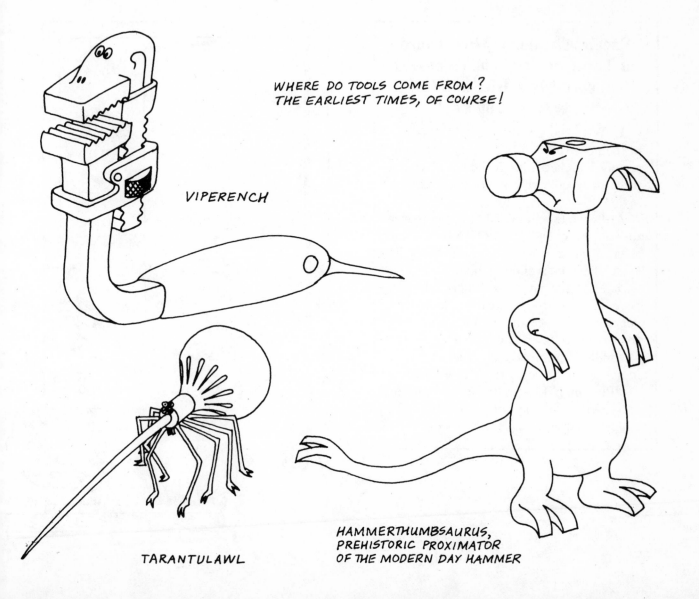

WHERE DO TOOLS COME FROM?
THE EARLIEST TIMES, OF COURSE!

VIPERENCH

TARANTULAWL

HAMMERTHUMBSAURUS,
PREHISTORIC PROXIMATOR
OF THE MODERN DAY HAMMER

Special Cautionary Procedure for Those of You Who Choose to Disregard My Advice and Use a Power Saw, You Fools

1. With the saw off and all the power in the house off and the power lines completely detached from the house, place the piece of wood you want to cut near the saw.

2. Leave the room and have the power turned back on. (WARNING: Never attempt to turn on the power yourself! Have one of your children do it.)

3. Have the power turned back off and peek into the room, wearing industrial goggles. If you see any signs of movement from the saw, fire a few rounds at it from a small-caliber revolver, such as you might use to unclog a toilet (see Chapter 4, "Plumbing"). If you see no signs of movement, have one of your remaining children retrieve the piece of wood.

The three major kinds of tools

● *Tools for hitting things to make them loose or to tighten up or jar their many complex, sophisticated electrical parts in such a manner that they function perfectly.* These are your hammers, maces, bludgeons, and truncheons.

● *Tools that, if dropped properly, can penetrate your foot.* Awls.

● *Tools that nobody should ever use because the potential danger is far greater than the value of any project that could possibly result.* Power saws, power drills, power staplers, any kind of tool that uses any kind of power more advanced than flashlight batteries.

How to get a complete home tool set for under four dollars

Go to one of those really cheap discount stores where they sell plastic furniture in colors visible from the planet Neptune and have a food section specializing in cardboard cartons full of Raisinets and malted milk balls manufactured during the Nixon administration. In either the Hardware or Housewares department, you'll find an item imported from an obscure oriental country and described as "Nine Tools in One," consisting of a little handle with interchangeable ends representing inscrutable oriental notions of tools that Americans might use around the home (see illustration). Buy it. This is the kind of tool set professionals use; not only is it inexpensive, but it also has a great safety feature not found in the so-called quality tool sets: The handle will actually break right off if you accidentally hit yourself or anything else, or expose it to direct sunlight.

WARNING: Do not be misled by advertisements for so-called tool sets allegedly containing large numbers of tools. These are frauds! Oh, sure, you get a lot of tools, but most of them are the same kind! For example, you'll get 127 wrenches, and the only difference is that one will be maybe an eighth of an inch bigger than another. Big deal.

UNIQUE!

OLS IN ONE BY KOX TOOLS

PRICE

$1.98

☆HAMMER

☆NEEDLE FOR THE INFLATION OF THE SOCCER OR FOOT BALLS

☆PAPER CLIP

☆TWO VERY DISTINCT SCREW DRIVERS OR CHISELS

☆SCISSORS

☆DEVICE TO FIND OUT: IS ELECTRICITY IN SOCKET ?

☆PLIERS WITH MOUTH THAT CHANGES

☆SANITARY TOOTH BRUSHES

Chapter 2

Wood

If God had wanted us to use it, He wouldn't have made plastic

Wood has been the preferred building material for thousands of years, because it is one of the few materials that will rot as well as burn. Basically, there are two kinds of wood: hardwoods such as oak and walnut, which are used by skilled craftsmen to make furniture that you cannot afford; and softwoods such as fir, spruce, and tripe, which are actually members of the crabgrass family and are more suitable to the kinds of projects that an incompetent such as yourself will be doing.

Dealing with lumberyards

Lumberyards are dangerous and hostile places, inhabited by suspicious men who wear bib overalls and spit a lot and duck behind piles of boards as soon as they see a homeowner coming. These men have lived in the lumberyard since childhood. It is the only home they know. At night, they just pull sheets of plywood over themselves and go to sleep. They don't like

Wood	Description	Uses
Pine	Sap-filled, unattractive	Rustic furniture, torches
Formica	Sort of like plastic, only less natural	Motel beds
Oak	Very heavy	Bridge parts
Rose-wood	Attractive, very durable	None
Chablis	Light, crisp	With chicken, fish
Balsa	Easy to lift	Trick furniture
Banyan	Swarming with tropical diseases	Religious statues

Handy Wood Chart

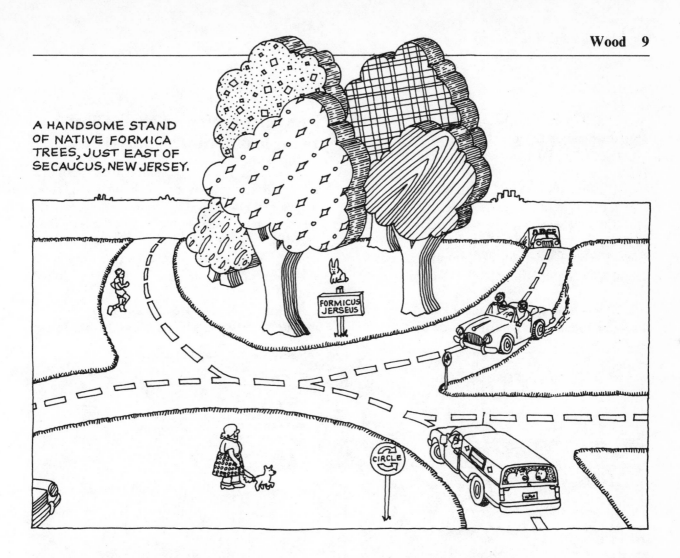

A HANDSOME STAND OF NATIVE FORMICA TREES, JUST EAST OF SECAUCUS, NEW JERSEY.

FORMICUS JERSEUS

CIRCLE

intruders, especially homeowners such as yourself who are buying wood for some idiot home project, and they will try any crafty ruse to drive you away. For example, all their wood measurements are lies. A so-called two-by-four is *not* two anythings by four anythings, and so on. There is no way you can possibly know what size of wood you're getting.

Another common trick among the lumbermen is to call things by silly names, such as "soffit." They dream these names up at night while they're lying under their sheets of plywood, and they use them to make you feel stupid when you try to order your wood.

YOU: Hi. I'd like two eight-foot two-by-fours, please.

LUMBERMAN: What are they for?

YOU: What?

LUMBERMAN: Are they for joists? Headers? Beams? Rafters? Footers? Sills? Framing? Tenons? Partitions? Templates? Easements? Debentures? Just what is it you want, mister?

YOU: Uh, well, ah, maybe I better go home and recheck my measurements.

The home center: an alternative to the lumberyard? *NO.*

Several years ago, some smart businessmen had an idea: Why not build a big store where a do-it-yourselfer could get everything he needed at reasonable prices? Then they decided, nah, the hell with it, let's build a home center. And before long home centers were springing up, like herpes, all over the United States.

Home centers are designed for the do-it-yourselfer who's willing to pay higher prices

for the convenience of being able to shop for lumber, hardware, and toasters all in one location. Notice I say "shop for," as opposed to "obtain." This is the major drawback of home centers: They are always out of everything except artificial Christmas trees. The home center employees have no time to reorder merchandise, because they are too busy applying little price stickers to every object—every board, washer, nail, and screw—in the entire store. Once they've applied a round of stickers, they immediately set out to apply a new set, with slightly higher prices, to the same merchandise. This leaves them no time to learn about the products they sell, so it is utterly futile to ask them for help.

Let's say a piece of your toilet breaks, so you remove the broken part, take it to the home center, and ask an employee if they carry replacements. The employee, who has never in his life even seen the inside of a toilet, will peer at the broken part in very much the same way that a member of a primitive Amazon jungle tribe would look at an electronic calculator, then say, "We're expecting a shipment of these sometime around the middle of next week."

So the bottom line is that home centers are even worse than lumberyards as a source for lumber. The only really good place to buy lumber is at a store where the lumber has already been cut and attached together in the form of furniture, finished, and put into boxes.

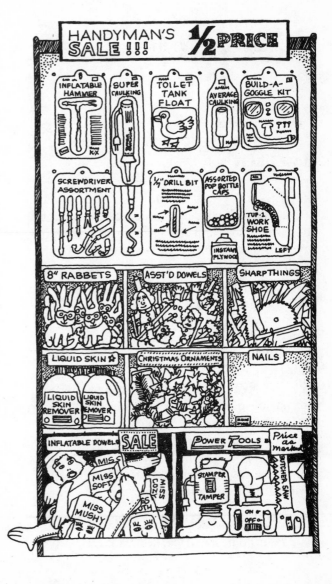

Chapter 3

Electricity

You can safely do your own wiring, most likely

Electricity is actually made up of extremely tiny particles, called electrons, that you cannot see with the naked eye unless you have been drinking. Electrons travel at the speed of light, which in most American homes is 110 volts per hour. This is very fast. In the time it has taken you to read this sentence so far, an electron could have traveled all the way from San Francisco to Hackensack, New Jersey, although God alone knows why it would want to.

The five main kinds of electricity are alternating current, direct current, lightning, static, and European. Most American homes have alternating current, which means that the electricity goes in one direction for a while, then goes the other direction. This prevents harmful electron buildup in the wires.

Your home electrical system

Your home electrical system is basically a bunch of wires that bring electricity into your home and take it back out before it has a chance to kill you. This is called a "circuit." The most common home electrical problem is when the circuit is broken by a "circuit breaker"; this causes the electricity to back up in one of the wires until it bursts out of an outlet in the form of sparks, which can damage your carpet. The best way to avoid broken circuits is to change your fuses regularly.

Another common problem is that the lights flicker. This sometimes means that your electrical system is inadequate, but more often it means that your home is possessed by demons, in which case you'll need to get a caulking gun and some caulking (see Chapter 6, "Heating and Cooling," for more on getting rid of demons with caulking.) If you're not sure whether your house is possessed, see *The Amityville Horror*, a fine documentary film based on an actual book. Or call in a licensed electrician, who is trained to spot the signs of demonic possession, such as blood coming down the stairs, enormous cats on the dinette table, etc.

CUTAWAY VIEW OF A TYPICAL ELECTRICAL SYSTEM

How to change a fuse

You should change your fuses every six months or 200,000 amperes, whichever comes first. Here's how:

1. Go down to the basement, which should be located beneath the first floor, and find the gray box with all kinds of wires leading to it and little stickers on it saying things like "CAUTION: 80 SKILLION WATTS."

2. Standing about 15 feet away, toss a small domestic animal toward the box and note whether it (a) falls to the floor unscathed or (b)

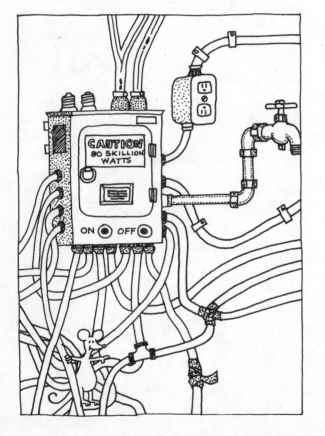
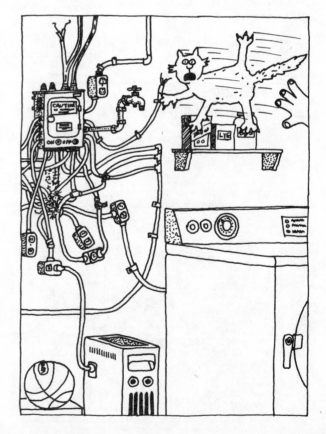

is reduced to a lump of carbon by a gigantic bolt of electricity.

3. In the event of (b), call an experienced electrician without dependents and have him replace your fuses. In the event of (a), open the box and remove the old fuses by unscrewing

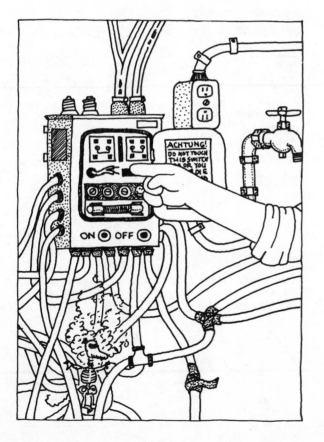

them or whacking at them with a ⅜-inch steel chisel, and replace them with new fuses, which can be obtained wherever new fuses are sold. Then simply close the box and continue to lead a normal life.

How to repair a broken electrical appliance

1. The primary cause of failure in electrical appliances is an expired warranty. Often, you can get an appliance running again simply by changing the warranty expiration date with a $^{37}/_{16}$-inch felt-tipped marker.

2. If this fails, take the appliance to the basement and leave it there for several months, on the theory that (a) it will get lonely and want to work again so it can be up in the kitchen with all the other appliances, or (b) we'll have a nuclear war, and you won't have any uses for appliances any more because you'll be too busy defending your beef jerky and water from your neighbors, or (c) you'll develop a horrible, lingering disease, and people will feel sorry for you and give you new appliances.

3. If, after several months, the appliance still doesn't work, locate the motor or some other electronic part and whap it briskly with a 58-ounce tire iron. This technique is particularly effective with your modern personal home electronic computers, which are smart enough

to not want to be struck by blunt instruments. Toasters are much, much stupider—some of them cannot perform even simple addition—and often must be whapped for hours before coming around.

Harness the power of nature to generate electricity for only pennies a day, not counting parts and labor

If you're tired of paying high electricity bills, and you live in an area that has a great deal of nature, you should definitely consider generating your own electricity via one of the extremely ecological methods described below. Then you should go back to whatever you were doing.

WIND POWER. Wind, which is imported into the United States from Canada in the form of cold air masses, can be used to turn the blades of a windmill, which in turn can generate electric power. At least that's what *Popular Mechanics* is always claiming. The big problem is that, because of labor problems, Canada is an unreliable source of wind. So what you need is a wind collection device, such as the Goodyear blimp, to store the wind for use during times of Canadian labor unrest.

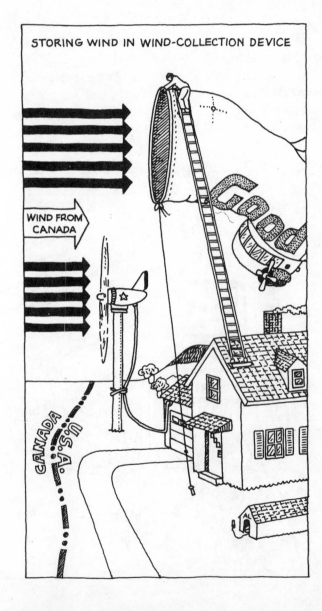

SEA POWER. The sea is potentially a source of vast amounts of electrical energy, as well as haddock. Scientists predict that some day, possibly as early as next week, whole cities will be powered by the sea. The key will be gigantic undersea electric turbines, whose blades will be turned by the relentless, powerful motion of lobsters walking along the sea bed. If you live near the sea and own a gigantic electric turbine, you can harness this power today. The trick is to make sure your turbine is parallel with the prevailing lobster motion.

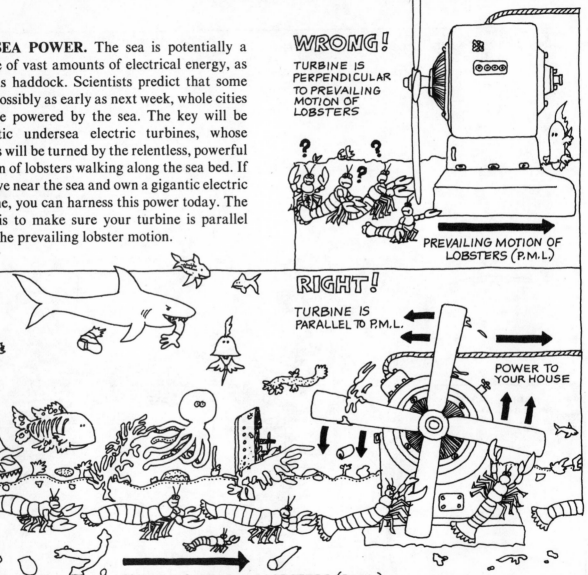

ATOMIC POWER. At one time atomic power was considered difficult to handle, but these days just about every dirtball little country has it, and I see no reason why you shouldn't, too. You'll need an atomic reactor. This is a good time to buy one: Most of your electric companies are trying to unload their reactors because they might have this defect wherein they heat up and go all the way through the earth and destroy Communist China, so you can probably pick one up for a song. Don't worry about the Communist Chinese. They're not losing any sleep over you, believe me.

Chapter 4

Plumbing

Troubleshooting your plumbing with a loaded sidearm

You should worry incessantly about your plumbing. No doubt you have heard the tragic story of the family who went away on vacation, unaware that one of their pipes had sprung a small leak. By the time they returned, the leak had destroyed the home and all their possessions, forcing them to collect $175,000 from the insurance company and use the money to go to Hawaii and buy a small, chic restaurant that became fabulously successful, so now all they do is lie around on the beach sipping tropical rum drinks.

This needless tragedy would never have occurred if this family had taken more of an interest in its plumbing. Plumbing is one of the easiest of do-it-yourself activities, requiring only a few simple tools and a willingness to stick your arm into a clogged toilet after a diseased houseguest has used it. In fact, you can solve many home plumbing problems, such as an annoying faucet drip, merely by turning up the radio. But before we get into any specific plumbing techniques, let's look at how plumbing works.

A plumbing system is very much like your electrical system, except that instead of electricity, it has water, and instead of wires, it has pipes, and instead of radios and waffle irons, it has faucets and toilets. So the truth is that your plumbing system is nothing at all like your electrical system, which is good, because electricity can kill you.

The major problem with plumbing systems is that they leak. To understand why, imagine that you're on a cross-country bus trip and you have drunk three six-packs of beer

TYPES OF HOUSEHOLD FIXTURES

PLUMBING   ELECTRICAL   MOTHER-IN-LAW

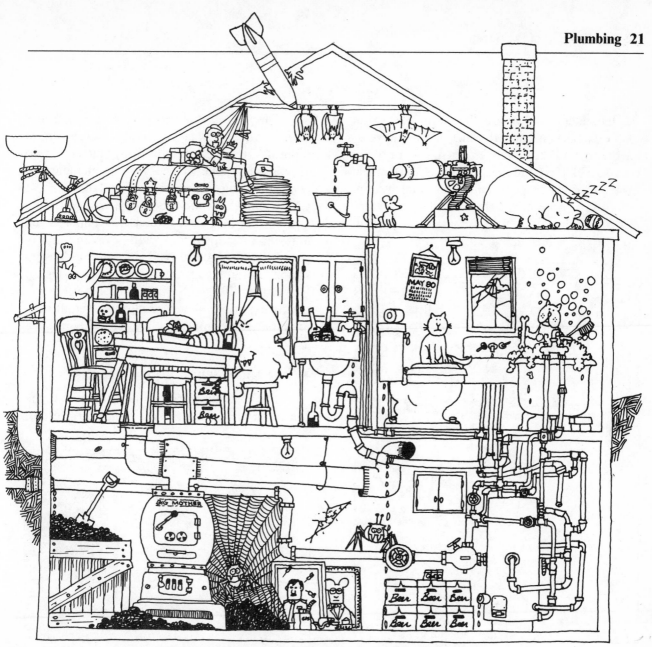

CUTAWAY VIEW OF A TYPICAL PLUMBING SYSTEM

singlehandedly and you really, really have to go to the bathroom, only the bus doesn't have a bathroom and the driver refuses to stop until he gets to Elkhart, Indiana, which is 280 miles away. That is how your home plumbing system feels all the time. It sits there filled with water, day in and day out, until after a while all it can think about is leaking.

The key to preventing leaks is proper maintenance. At least once a year (and more often if you have a small brain) you should go around and poke at the various elements of your plumbing system with the end of a cane. If you see anything the least bit suspicious, make a note of it in a spiral notebook. This routine maintenance program will prevent many plumbing headaches. And if anything does go wrong, don't be afraid to tackle it yourself! Remember: The only difference between you and an experienced master plumber is that he is an experienced master plumber, whereas you are not.

What to do when a pipe breaks

1. Go down to the dankest corner of the basement and locate the valve that turns off all

TESTING A PIPE FOR LEAKS

LOCATING YOUR WATER VALVE

the water in the house. This will be the valve that is covered with slime and a spiderweb containing a spider and the festering bodies of dead insects.

    2. Using a ¾-inch drive socket wrench or

a tire iron, prod the spider firmly until it scuttles off to some other area of the basement, muttering angrily.

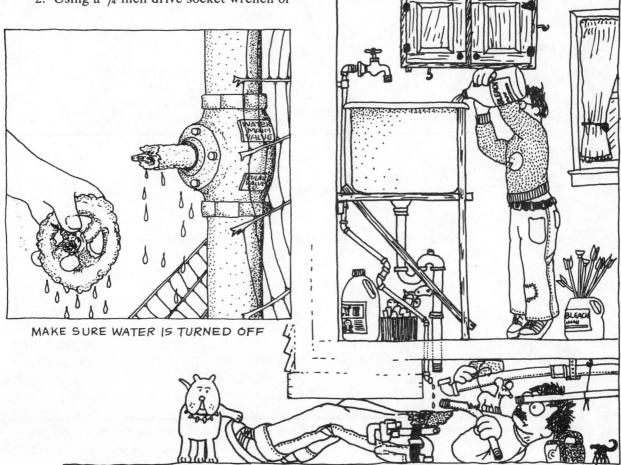

MAKE SURE WATER IS TURNED OFF

YOU MAY HAVE TO ASSIST THE PLUMBER, IF NECESSARY

3. Turn the valve handle clockwise until it breaks off in your hand like a damp pretzel, which is the signal that the water is off.

4. Locate the broken pipe and replace it with a new pipe in such a manner that it will not leak even when it has water going through it.

5. Have a plumber turn the water back on. This job is best left to a professional, since (a) the handle is broken off and (b) the spider has returned with thousands of poisonous friends and relatives to defend the valve. Be sure to select a plumber who has a good reputation and life insurance and a flamethrower.

SWEATING A PIPE

The history of the toilet

The toilet was invented several hundred years ago by Sir Robert Toilet, an Englishman who was trying to put an end to war. At the time, everybody went to the bathroom outdoors, which, as you can imagine, was fairly disgusting. So countries were always trying to go to the bathroom in other countries. Thousands of, say, Frenchmen would suddenly appear in Germany, relieve themselves, and stride back to France, snickering; the next day even greater numbers of Germans would retaliate. Eventually the dispute would escalate into a war, which was even worse, because of the horses.

SIR ROBERT INTRODUCES HIS INVENTION

Then, thankfully, Sir Robert had his idea: Instead of going to the bathroom on the ground in other countries, why not go to the bathroom in a toilet? This would put an end to needless wars and give everybody a chance to read magazines. The idea caught on, and today very few wars are caused by the French and the Germans going to the bathroom on each other's land, which is not to say that they don't want to.

Three Useful Tips for Unclogging a Clogged Toilet

● Before you attempt to unclog the toilet, make sure that it is a toilet that you are responsible for. If it is in a public restroom, or someone else's home, don't give it another thought. Just sidle out of the room as if nothing has happened.

● If the clog is caused by something soft, such as a corsage, you can dislodge it simply by firing a .22-caliber pistol into the toilet.

● For tougher clogs, such as turtles or jewelry, you'll need to flush a lit cherry bomb, which you can obtain from any reliable teenager.

Chapter 5

Walls

Paneling, and other common mistakes

Walls are an important part of any home, because they keep the roof from falling down and damaging your television set. But walls are more than just structural; they are also large objects that you have to cover with something. The three major wall coverings, in ascending order of unattractiveness, are paint, wallpaper, and paneling.

How to paint a room

1. To determine how much paint you'll need, stand with your back against an end wall of the room you plan to paint, then take little mincing steps across the room until you mince into the opposite wall. Now repeat the procedure, only start with your back against a side wall. Now multiply the number of steps by the length of your foot in inches, making sure you subtract for windows. This will tell you the number of square inches your floor would be if it had windows in it.

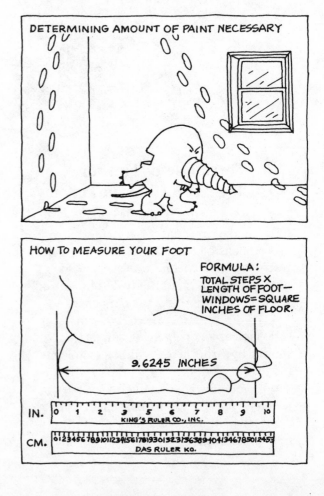

DETERMINING AMOUNT OF PAINT NECESSARY

HOW TO MEASURE YOUR FOOT

FORMULA:
TOTAL STEPS X LENGTH OF FOOT— WINDOWS = SQUARE INCHES OF FLOOR.

9.6245 INCHES

IN. 0 1 2 3 4 5 6 7 8 9 10
KING'S RULER CO., INC.

CM. 0123456789101112314151617181930152313638940413467850124523
DAS RULER KO.

2. Go to a paint store and buy six gallons of paint. Oil-based paint is tough and adheres extremely well to any surface, especially human skin. Your best bet is latex paint, which comes in a wide variety of colors, all of them white. Well, almost white. Paint manufacturers have tried for years to make plain white paint, but unfortunately their factories are old and unsanitary, and the paint batches always end up getting contaminated with rodent droppings. So all the paint comes out off-white, and they have to give it classy names like Oyster White or Antique White (see box), on the grounds that nobody would buy it if they called it Rodent Dropping White.

3. Now it's time to paint. Read the directions on the paint can, which will contain some snotty statement such as "CAUTION: SUR-

---

Manufacturers' Aliases for Not-Really-White Paint, with Percentages of Rodent Droppings in Parentheses

Antique White (0.2%)

Oyster White (0.4%)

Cottage Cheese White (1.4%)

Urinal White (2.7%)

Clam White (3.8%)

Nasal Spray Container White (6.3%)

Whale Blubber White (11.2%)

Phlegm White (39.5%)

Lobster White (87.9%)

Cottage Cheese after Six Weeks of Sitting in an Unrefrigerated Place White (144.5%)

FACE MUST BE FREE OF DIRT, GREASE, AND PEELING OR FLAKING PAINT." This is utter nonsense, of course. If the surface were free of dirt, grease, and peeling or flaking paint, why on earth would you want to paint it? So don't waste any time preparing the surface. Go ahead and paint the damn surface, dirt and all. If you see any insects, paint over them, too, unless they are major tropical insects, in which case you should first smash them flat with a 23-ounce rubber-tipped mallet, such as your professional painters use.

Wallpaper

Wallpaper dates back to colonial times, when people had much smaller brains. It would have died out years ago if not for the fact that women get pregnant. Pregnancy causes women to secrete a hormone that compels them to want to install wallpaper with jungle animals

RIGHT

WRONG

WRONG

on it in the baby's room. My wife and I installed jungle-animal wallpaper on a hot August day when she was about 17 months pregnant, and she was a driven woman. She was determined to make the head of the rhinoceros on one sheet of wallpaper line up with the rhinoceros body on the adjacent sheet. Proper rhinoceros alignment is very important to your child's development. Children who grow up looking at rhinoceros heads springing out of, say, clown bodies, are likely to grow up to become drug addict ax murderers or members of the state legislature.

The easy way to wallpaper a room

Don't be an idiot. There is no easy way to wallpaper a room. The finest scientific minds in the nation have been working on this problem for decades, and they have failed miserably. Oh, sure, the salesman at the wallpaper store will tell you it's easy to install wallpaper, but you'll notice his store walls aren't wallpapered. They're painted Rodent Dropping White.

Paneling

Paneling is a surprisingly easy way to make any room less attractive. A panel is simply a four-by-eight-foot piece of compressed industrial waste that has been finished in such a way that it looks nothing whatsoever like wood, then given an absurd name such as

Heritage Oak. If you were to show a typical piece of paneling to 100 people chosen at random, and ask them what it was, they would all answer, "I don't know, but it's not wood."

Many homeowners panel their basements, because basement walls are usually cold, dank concrete with earthworms oozing through the cracks. The idea is that if you put paneling up, you'll transform your basement into a warm, friendly recreation room where the family can play bumper pool and have several hours of meaningful family togetherness until the earthworms start oozing through the cracks between the panels.

Paneling Tips

● The shiny, plasticlike side of the paneling should always face the inside of the room, unless you think the unfinished industrial-waste side is more attractive.

● The easiest way to install paneling is to simply lean it up against the walls all around the room. This way, you can remove it quickly and hide it in the garage when tasteful visitors come to call.

● If you decide to attach the panels permanently, you may have to adjust them slightly to allow for doors and windows, assuming you intend to continue to use the doors and windows.

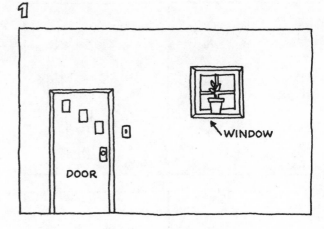

UNPANELED WALL

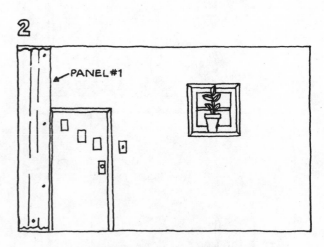

PANEL #1 INSTALLED

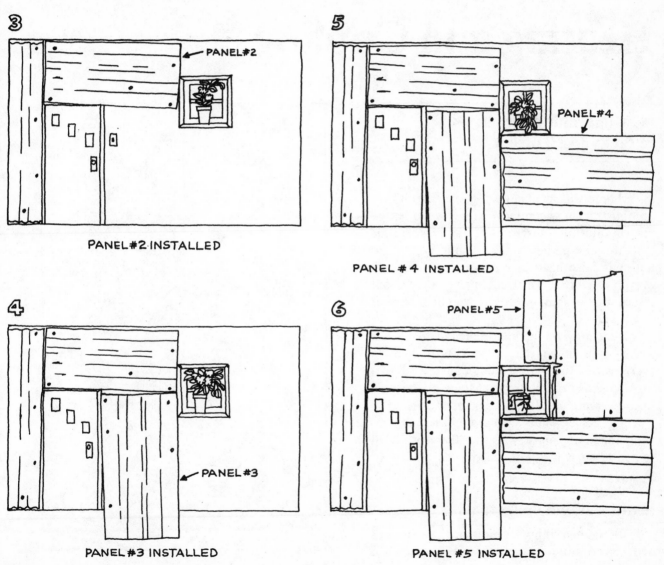

3

PANEL#2

PANEL#2 INSTALLED

4

PANEL#3

PANEL#3 INSTALLED

5

PANEL#4

PANEL #4 INSTALLED

6

PANEL#5

PANEL #5 INSTALLED

Chapter 6

Heating and Cooling

New-age, chic alternatives to tacky fossil fuels

There was a time, during the Eisenhower administration, when most homes were heated via thermostats. Just one of these wondrous little devices, no larger than a snuff box, could automatically heat an entire house. This left everybody with lots of free time to worry about international communism or watch "Leave It to Beaver."

You may be fortunate enough to have a 1950s-style home that is still heated by a thermostat. If so, you should count your blessings, because many, many homes in the past decade were built by deranged granola-oriented ecology nuts who are opposed to convenience in any form, and who therefore tried to heat their homes with wood.

Wood heat: inefficient, but dangerous

Wood heat is highly ecological, since trees are a renewable resource. If you cut down a

CUTAWAY VIEW OF A TYPICAL HEATING SYSTEM   CUTAWAY VIEW OF A TYPICAL COOLING SYSTEM

What to Do about a Cold, Drafty Room

No matter what kind of heating system you have, you'll probably find that one room always feels cold and drafty. The commonest cause of this problem is demonic possession. Demons are always taking over rooms and making them colder. This is annoying, but it's a heck of a lot better than when they take over bodies and turn their heads around backwards or make them speak dead languages, the way they did to that little girl in *The Exorcist.*

If you want to get rid of the demons, you'll need a caulking gun and some caulking. Clear out a space in the middle of the floor of the possessed room, and squeeze the caulking onto the floor in a mystical, demon-repelling pattern, as shown here. The good news is that this will cause the demon to stop possessing the room. The bad news is that it will be looking for something else to possess, so be alert if you find your head is rotating like a bar stool.

tree, another will grow in its place. And if you cut down the new tree, still another will grow. And if you cut down that tree, yet another will grow, only this one will be a mutation with long, poisonous tentacles and revenge in its heart, and it will sit there in the forest, cackling and making elaborate plans for when you come back.

To heat your house with wood, you'll need a good wood source. The best wood sources are woodpiles, which can be found in most suburban backyards in early fall. You should gather your wood very early in the morning, wearing dark clothing and a loaded sidearm. You should try to gather hardwoods, such as veneer, because these extinguish themselves automatically seconds after you light them, which makes them very safe. You should avoid the softwoods, such as cork, because these burn far too easily. You can cause a piece of softwood to explode into flame merely by dropping it on the ground.

The principle behind wood heat is that wood contains a certain number of British Thermal Units, or Btu's. Btu's are these little thermal units invented by the British to tell you how much heat you have in your wood, and like everything else invented by the British, they don't work. Let's say you have a log made of oak. Now a British person would claim that you're going to get maybe 10,000 Btu's of heat when you burn your log, but in fact you're

going to get 6 Btu's of heat and 9,994 Btu's of smoke. This is why virtually everyone in England wears sweaters all the time.

Now you'll need someplace to burn your wood. You should not use your fireplace, because scientists now believe that, contrary to popular opinion, fireplaces actually remove heat from houses. Really, that's what scientists believe. In fact, many scientists actually use their fireplaces to cool their houses in the summer. If you visit a scientist's house on a sultry August day, you'll find a cheerful fire roaring on the hearth and the scientist sitting nearby, remarking on how cool he is and drinking heavily.

Instead of a fireplace, you should heat your house with a woodstove, preferably one that is airtight. To test for airtightness, leave a smallish animal that your children have not grown fond of, such as a chicken, inside the stove for several days. You can use the chicken later to clean your chimney.

Wood-burning stoves are large, squat, black objects that range widely in price from $500 to $525 and come in a variety of attractive styles designed to enhance the appearance of any room whose appearance would be enhanced by the presence of a large, squat, black object. Your stove must be installed safely, so this is something you should leave in the hands of somebody who will charge you a great deal of money. But once it's installed,

your stove will give you hours of comfort and enjoyment, unless you burn wood in it, in which case it will give you hours of smoke and fear caused by the fact that you have an insanely hot metal object in your living room.

Heating your home with solar energy

Solar heat comes from the sun, which is really nothing more than a nearby star, which means it could explode at any minute. In the meantime, though, the sun is giving off scads of energy in the form of rays, which slam into the Earth at nearly the speed of light and bounce back into outer space, where they illuminate the moon, form comets, etc. But you can also use these rays to form heat. If you were to capture just one-billionth of the rays that hit your house every day, all your appliances would melt.

The easiest way to heat your house with solar energy is to move it to Central America, which is located directly under the sun. You'll start feeling much, much warmer in a matter of minutes, and you'll never complain about high fuel bills again. You'll be too busy fending off tarantulas the size of briefcases.

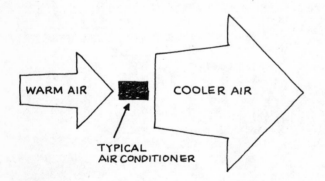

WARM AIR → TYPICAL AIR CONDITIONER → COOLER AIR

Air conditioners

All air conditioners work essentially the same way: They take warm air and make it cooler somehow, as the illustration shows. If your air conditioner fails to operate properly,

the chances are that one or more parts is broken. To repair it, you should take it to the basement and hit it (see Chapter 3, "Electricity").

Heat pumps

Heat pumps are a new wrinkle on the heating and cooling scene: in the summer, they cool your home, and in the winter, they heat it! How is this possible? Heat pump manufacturers tell us the secret is that even on the coldest day, there is some heat in the outside air, and the heat pump extracts this heat. This is a lie, of course. There is no heat in the air on cold days. That's why we call them "cold days." If there's so much heat out there on cold days, how come you never see heat pump manufacturers frolicking outside in bathing suits, huh? Answer me that.

The truth is that heat pumps work via theft. Even on the coldest days, there is heat in your neighbors' houses. The heat pump sucks up this heat, like some kind of gigantic electrical leech, and uses it to keep you warm. On a really cold day, your heat pump may have to range for miles to keep you warm; it will steal heat from churches, old peoples' homes, orphanages, hospitals, etc. It will even suck the heat out of newly born puppies. This is definitely the high-tech heat source of the future. You should get one before your neighbor does.

Chapter 7

Insulation and Weatherproofing

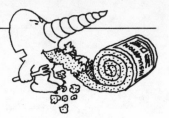

Kicking the crutches out from under Old Man Winter

During the winter, heated air is constantly escaping from your home. During the summer, cooled air is constantly escaping from your home. If you had a brain in your head, you'd get the hell out of your home before you die of oxygen deprivation.

Your other option is insulation.

Even though insulation is one of the most important and boring issues of the day, many people don't know how it works. I certainly don't. I have read dozens of articles about how to insulate and weather-strip my home, and they're all full of terms I don't understand, like this: "When caulking your windows, be sure to put a ⅛-inch bead of polyvinyl-butylacetate caulking between the jamb and the main soffit adjacent to the eave cornice, taking care not to dislodge the newels."

Now I have looked at my windows, and I cannot for the life of me locate any of these things. All I have in my windows are pieces of

wood and poisonous spiders. I don't have the vaguest idea where to put the caulking. This is a problem because, as you have probably noticed, caulking guns are designed so that as soon as you pick them up, the caulking starts oozing out, and it keeps on oozing out until there is none left. This is a clever ploy of the caulking manufacturers to keep themselves in business.

So anyway, I end up standing outside my window, looking for the eave cornice, with caulking oozing onto my pants, until finally I give up and smear some caulking on the spiders and go inside.

So I thought, as a public service, I would explain home insulation in layman's terms. I will do it in the handy question-and-answer format in which I make up questions and then answer them, which is a heck of a lot easier than answering real questions.

Eight common stupid questions about insulation

Q: Where should I put insulation?

A: Wherever you can work comfortably. The worst place is the attic, because attics are

hot, dangerous places, full of filthy objects and rabid bats. Oh, I know do-it-yourself home insulation articles always have pictures showing a cheerful homeowner cheerfully insulating his attic, but these pictures are frauds. I mean, look at the attic they show: It always looks clean, well lit, and safe, unlike any other attic in the known world. What those articles don't tell you is that when the pictures were taken, dozens of highly trained men were standing just out of camera range, holding the bats at bay with semiautomatic rifles. So stay out of your attic. Put your insulation someplace safe and convenient, such as in your den or along your driveway.

Q: What kind of insulation should I buy?

A: You should definitely not buy synthetic insulation, which comes in grotesque colors and is harsh and scratchy and leaves you covered with prickly little things that will never come off as long as you live. I suggest you buy insulation that is naturally soft and washable and can be dyed to match your den decor. Cotton is a good choice.

Q: How much insulation do I need?
A: Four thousand dollars' worth.

Q: What about blown-in insulation?
A: Blown-in insulation is fine, if you don't

mind a fuzzy tongue and wads of spit-covered insulation all over the place.

Q: How does insulation work?

A: To understand how insulation works, conduct this simple home experiment.

1. Mix yourself a stiff gin and tonic in a tall glass, then drink it. Notice how cold the glass feels? Repeat this procedure several times, until you have a really good idea how cold the glass feels.

2. Now wrap a piece of insulation around the glass and pour yourself several more gin and tonics and drink them. Notice how much warmer the glass feels? Even your stomach feels warmer, doesn't it?

3. Repeat the procedure several times,

and you'll start having all kinds of major insights about insulation. It also works fairly well on the Middle East crisis.

Q: Do I actually have to install the insulation in my house to qualify for the federal tax credit?

A: No. You can leave it in your garage, or, if you prefer, simply toss it out of your car window on the way home from the insulation store.

Q: What is "R-value"?

A: I don't know. It was one of those things that were in vogue back during the 1970s, like disco and the metric system, but you hardly ever hear anybody talk about it any more, so I wouldn't worry about it. I don't think it's suspected of causing cancer or anything.

Q: What about dirt?

A: Dirt is a superb natural insulator. It is not mere coincidence that the Amazon jungle, which is filthy, is one of the warmest places on Earth. During the great energy crises of the 1970s, many smart, energy-conscious, patriotic homeowners stopped cleaning their houses or bathing or even wiping off the slime that grows around the base of the toilet, and today their heating bills are extremely low, although I should point out that they spend an average of $65,000 a year on antibiotics.

Caulking Doors and Windows

Energy experts tell us that caulking doors and windows is one of the easiest ways to get caulking all over yourself. Here's how you do it:

1. Take a good, close look around the edges of your front door. See all those tiny cracks? Ignore them. I mean, why waste your time on tiny cracks? It's the door hole (the hole that appears in your house when you open the door) that you should be worrying about. Old Man Winter isn't going to mess around with cracks when he can just waltz through the door hole.

2. Go to your home center or hardware store and get a caulking gun and enough caulking to plug your door and window holes. A typical door hole will require 750 tubes of caulking, but you'll save so much energy that the caulking job will easily pay for itself by the time the Earth establishes permanent colonies on the planet Jupiter.

3. Apply the caulking in such a manner that Old Man Winter will be unable to waltz through the door hole.

Chapter 8

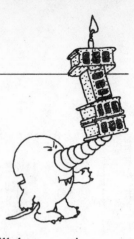

Masonry

At last, a practical use for Maine

"Masonry" is a term used in the building profession to describe any kind of building material that can fall on you and kill you. The big advantage of masonry structures is that they last thousands of years; the only real drawback is that they eventually become haunted. The two most popular projects for do-it-yourselfers are walls and pyramids.

How to build a wall

1. Drive two stakes into the ground and stretch a string between them to serve as a guide for where your wall will be.*
2. Attach a row of bricks or other masonry units to your string. Always start from the top, so your wall will have a nice, even appearance.
3. Using cement or masking tape, attach a second layer of masonry units under the first, and so on, forming tasteful and traditional masonry patterns. Do not remove the string until your wall reaches all the way to the ground.

An easy home pyramid in three steps

Some do-it-yourselfers hesitate to build pyramids because they have been led to believe it is extremely difficult. The blame for this widespread misconception has to rest squarely on the shoulders of archeologists, who are always announcing in loud voices that they don't have the vaguest notion how the Great Pyramids of Egypt were built. Well, of course

---

*Despite what many so-called professionals will tell you, your string should *not* be level with respect to the horizon. You probably can't even see the horizon from where you live, so the hell with it. Your string should be level with respect to the *ground*. This principle was discovered thousands of years ago by the ancient Chinese when they built the Great Wall of China to keep out the marauding barbarian hordes. If the ancient Chinese had been so stupid as to build the Great Wall parallel to the horizon, the barbarians would have been able to barge right into China. So the Chinese wisely built the wall parallel to the ground, which stopped the barbarians. Of course, the ancient Chinese were fortunate that the barbarians weren't bright enough to simply throw a few ladders together and climb over the wall, but that's why they were called barbarians. All they knew how to do was maraud around in hordes, and as often as not they got *that* wrong. The bottom line is that there is a right way and a wrong way to stretch your string, and you should stretch it the right way.

BARBARIANS WOULD HAVE OVERRUN CHINA IF THE GREAT WALL HAD BEEN CONSTRUCTED LEVEL WITH THE HORIZON. INSTEAD, THESE MARAUDERS WERE KEPT OUT WITH THE GROUND-HUGGING STRUCTURE WE KNOW TODAY (INSET).

they don't. They're archeologists, for God's sake. When the rest of us were learning useful skills, they were out squatting on some wretched desert somewhere digging up little snippets of ancient pottery and trying to glue them together so as to form ancient pots. They wouldn't know how to seal a Tupperware container, let alone build a pyramid.

I have personally conducted a very thorough study of a photograph of a pyramid in the *Encyclopaedia Britannica,* and I have concluded that the ancient Egyptians built them by piling up a lot of great big stones in the shape of a pyramid. I see nothing particularly difficult about this, and I encourage all of you to rush right out and build a pyramid according to the instructions below.

MATERIALS

- 50,000 hewing tools
- A source of rocks, such as the coast of Maine
- 150,000 college students. College students are perfect for pyramid building, because they're strong and they're used to engaging in elaborate, pointless mass activities, such as attending college.

DIRECTIONS

1. Line up your students and have them count off by threes to form three teams, the

HEWER   HAULER   HEFTER

Hewers, the Haulers, and the Hefters. Encourage the teams to make up team cheers and play pranks on each other and stick their fingers in the air and yell "We're Number One!" so as to build a sense of college-style fun that will make them work without food or water until they drop.

2. Position your Hewers on the coast of Maine and have them hew it into large blocks of stone, each about the size of a bungalow, which your Haulers should haul to your pyramid site.

NOTE: Maine probably has a Department of Environmental Activities or some other ecology-nut organization that will come up with all kinds of picky reasons why it's illegal to remove the coast, so the police may try to stop one of your blocks as the Haulers inch it toward the state line. Under no circumstances should your Haulers try to outrun the police, because once you get a gigantic stone block going three or four miles an hour it becomes very difficult to control, which could lead to major damage in the form of hernias. A much better approach is to disguise the stone blocks as Rose Bowl parade-style floats, which are perfectly logical objects for college students to be hauling around, and thus unlikely to make the police suspicious.

3. Have your Hefters form the blocks into a pyramid full of hidden passageways and vaults containing ancient dead Egyptians and invaluable art objects. It might help if you provided the Hefters with a pyramid-shaped string stretched between two stakes, as shown here, but don't feel that you have to. You've done enough already.

Chapter 9

Easy Projects

Getting off to a slow start

Here are a few beginner's projects for do-it-yourselfers, or even craftsmen who have become heavily dependent upon narcotic substances. The first weds two boards together in a way that is not only attractive, but also highly practical around the home.

Project #1: Two boards attached together

MATERIALS

● 1 board, preferably wooden, 11′ 13/18″ × 45/32″ × 7′ 4 15/15″ or some other size
● 1 drop of the glue that is advertised on television as being capable of lifting a domestic automobile

TOOLS

● Various saws or axes such as you might use to divide a board into 2 separate boards so you can attach them together again in the form of a project
● A stubby, craftsmanlike pencil

DIRECTIONS

1. Look down one edge of the board in a highly critical manner, as you have seen professional carpenters do. If you see anything in the least bit suspicious, report it to the police immediately.

2. Using a copy of *Newsweek* magazine as a guide, draw a line across the board with your pencil.

3. Carefully whack the board on or near the line with an ax or saw until it is actually 2 boards.

4. Use your glue to assemble your project as illustrated. Be very careful in handling the glue, so as not to permit your project to become permanently bonded to your head.

OPTIONAL SAFETY DEVICE

To prevent injury from the jagged board edges, install a rubber glove on each end.

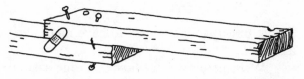

TWO BOARDS ATTACHED TOGETHER (DETAIL VIEW)

PROJECT WITH OPTIONAL SAFETY DEVICES
INSTALLED ON EACH END

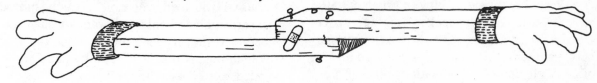

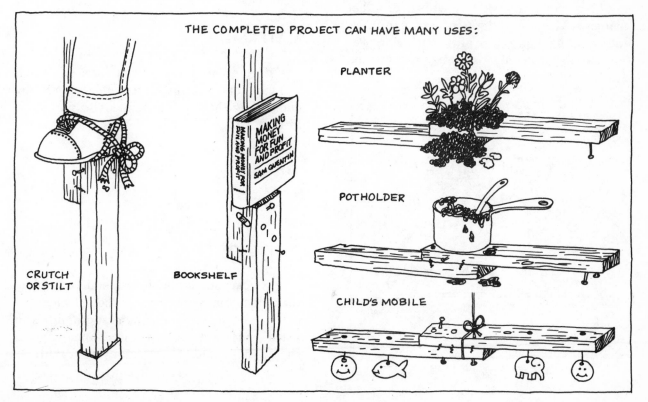

THE COMPLETED PROJECT CAN HAVE MANY USES:

PLANTER

POTHOLDER

CHILD'S MOBILE

CRUTCH
OR STILT

BOOKSHELF

MAKING
MONEY
FOR FUN
AND PROFIT
SAM QUENTIN

Project #2: A highly modular and portable total home storage system made from industrial refuse

Probably the single biggest problem in the entire world today is lack of storage space. Look at Asia. From what I read in the newspapers, I gather Asia has all these huddled masses of people teeming around with no place to store anything, and everybody is wretched. I bet your own home is no different; you can never find anything, and you're always tripping over things. This is mainly because you drink too much, but it wouldn't hurt to have more storage space.

Well, here's a total home storage system that will easily hold every object and domestic animal you own, yet can be easily moved or disassembled should you want to burn it. The secret is that it has a modern modular design, which means that it is actually packing crates piled on top of each other.

MATERIALS

• A great many packing crates, which you can obtain at any large factory merely by demanding them at gunpoint. Also pick up a forklift.

TOOLS

• A cattle prod

DIRECTIONS

Stack your crates in a modular fashion, then place your possessions in them, using your cattle prod to keep your domestic animals in place and ward off law enforcement agents should they attempt to reclaim your forklift.

HUDDLED ASIAN MASSES

Project #3: Cutting board/ platform bed

Homeowners constantly complain, "I have room for a cutting board *or* a platform bed, but not both." If that sounds like you, then this project is just what the doctor ordered. By day, it's a cutting board that's spacious enough for all your cutting needs, including whole roast oxen. By night, it's a modern, hippie-style platform bed that combines the advantages of simple design with the advantages of sleeping on the floor.

MATERIALS

- A sheet of plywood

TOOLS

- An industrial-grade spatula

DIRECTIONS

1. Assemble the plywood.
2. To use the project as a cutting board, simply place it in an attractive kitchen location and cut things on it.
3. To convert it to a platform bed, simply flip it over and place it on the floor.
4. To convert it back to a cutting board, use the spatula to pry it off the floor, which it will be attached to by congealed oxen blood.

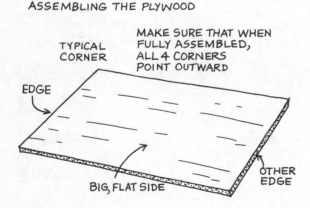

ASSEMBLING THE PLYWOOD

TYPICAL CORNER

MAKE SURE THAT WHEN FULLY ASSEMBLED, ALL 4 CORNERS POINT OUTWARD

EDGE

BIG, FLAT SIDE

OTHER EDGE

CUTTING BOARD USAGE

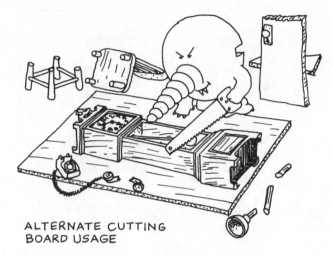

ALTERNATE CUTTING
BOARD USAGE

PLATFORM BED

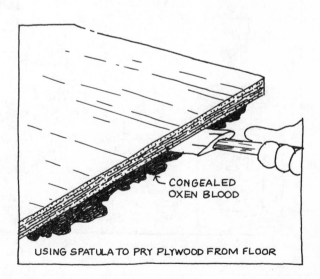

CONGEALED
OXEN BLOOD

USING SPATULA TO PRY PLYWOOD FROM FLOOR

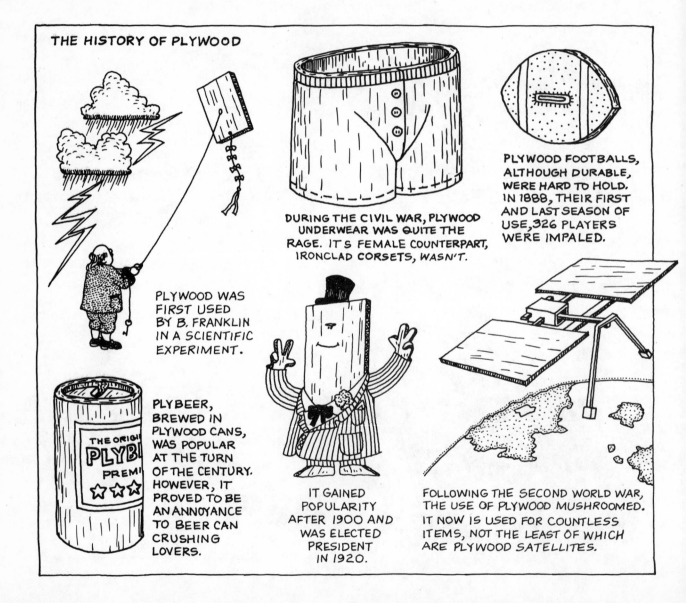

THE HISTORY OF PLYWOOD

PLYWOOD WAS FIRST USED BY B. FRANKLIN IN A SCIENTIFIC EXPERIMENT.

DURING THE CIVIL WAR, PLYWOOD UNDERWEAR WAS QUITE THE RAGE. IT'S FEMALE COUNTERPART, IRONCLAD CORSETS, WASN'T.

PLYWOOD FOOTBALLS, ALTHOUGH DURABLE, WERE HARD TO HOLD. IN 1888, THEIR FIRST AND LAST SEASON OF USE, 326 PLAYERS WERE IMPALED.

PLYBEER, BREWED IN PLYWOOD CANS, WAS POPULAR AT THE TURN OF THE CENTURY. HOWEVER, IT PROVED TO BE AN ANNOYANCE TO BEER CAN CRUSHING LOVERS.

IT GAINED POPULARITY AFTER 1900 AND WAS ELECTED PRESIDENT IN 1920.

FOLLOWING THE SECOND WORLD WAR, THE USE OF PLYWOOD MUSHROOMED. IT NOW IS USED FOR COUNTLESS ITEMS, NOT THE LEAST OF WHICH ARE PLYWOOD SATELLITES.

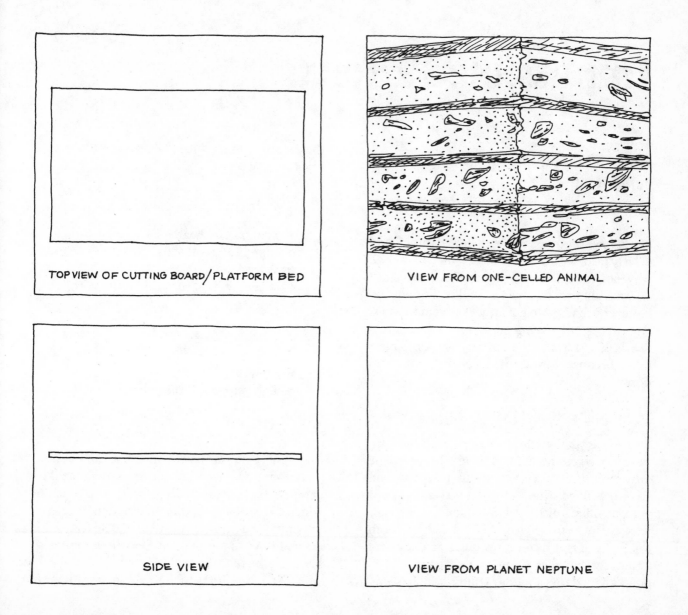

TOP VIEW OF CUTTING BOARD/PLATFORM BED

VIEW FROM ONE-CELLED ANIMAL

SIDE VIEW

VIEW FROM PLANET NEPTUNE

Chapter 10

Impossible Projects

How to build a hot tub and a hotter computer

Now that you've built the simple and utterly useless starter projects in Chapter 9, why not tackle these two advanced projects? One reason that springs to mind is that nobody has ever been able to get either of them to work. Another is the likelihood of serious injury or death. If you need any more reasons, drop me a note, because I'm sure I can come up with dozens.

Project #1: Easy-to-build hot tub

Have you ever wondered what makes Californians so calm? Besides drugs, I mean. The answer is hot tubs. A hot tub is a redwood container filled with water that you sit in naked with members of the opposite sex who are not necessarily your spouse. After a few hours in their hot tubs, Californians don't give a damn about earthquakes or mass murderers. They don't give a damn about anything, which is why

they are able to produce "Laverne and Shirley" week after week.

MATERIALS

- Footers and headers
- Many redwood slats
- Water
- A couple hundred gallons of Clorox
- Penicillin

TOOLS

- Shovel
- Tub-making implements

DIRECTIONS

I suggest you locate your hot tub outside your house, so it won't do too much damage if it catches fire or explodes. First, you decide which direction your hot tub should face for maximum solar energy. After much trial and error, I have found that the best direction for a hot tub to face is up.

The next step is to dig the footers. I'm not

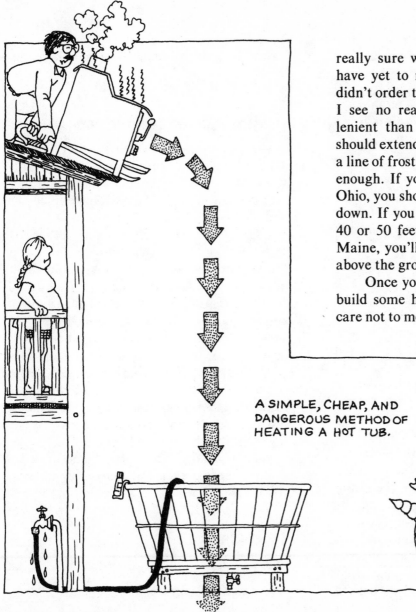

A SIMPLE, CHEAP, AND DANGEROUS METHOD OF HEATING A HOT TUB.

really sure why hot tubs need footers, but I have yet to read a do-it-yourself article that didn't order the reader to dig a few footers, and I see no reason why I should be any more lenient than the other writers. Your footers should extend down to the "frost line," which is a line of frost that you'll come to if you dig deep enough. If you live in a normal state, such as Ohio, you should find the frost line about 2 feet down. If you live in Florida, you'll have to dig 40 or 50 feet to find any frost; if you live in Maine, you'll find your frost line 10 to 12 feet above the ground, almost any time of year.

Once you've dug your footers, you should build some headers and several joists, taking care not to mortise the soffits. Now all you have to do is get a large quantity of redwood slats and attach them together in such a manner that they form a watertight tub, and you're all set to go . . . except that now you need some way to get water into the tub and heat it.

Contrary to what a lot of so-called experts will tell you, you don't need fancy plumbing and a filtering system for your hot tub. All you need to do is fill it up with the garden hose, or used dishwater. This approach is much cheaper and the only drawback is that after a couple of days the water will teem with every known form of deadly mutant disease-causing micro-organism. So if you're a real health fanatic, you might want to test the tub before you use it by tossing in a cat or a neighbor's child. If neither of these is available, you might want to pour in a couple of hundred gallons of Clorox mixed with penicillin just to be on the safe side.

The only other question is how you're going to heat your outdoor hot tub once the cool fall weather rolls around. One method that we have found to be simple, cheap, and dangerous is the wood-burning stove. What we do is perch the stove on a ledge above the hot tub, get it up to about 36,000 degrees Fahrenheit, then tip it over into the tub. In a matter of seconds, the water that was once merely tepid is warm enough to vaporize stainless steel, and many of the deadly mutant disease-causing microorganisms are dead. Of course, the ones that survive are usually very angry, so it's best to wait a week or two before you actually plunge in.

Project #2: Homemade computer

Despite what you've heard from computer salesmen, home computers are actually straightforward devices that can be built in an afternoon by anyone who has a few simple tools and the brains of a spittoon.

Once you have gained some experience with your computer, you can program it to do the kinds of things that computers owned by major corporations do, such as destroy the credit ratings of people you don't even know, or answer your telephone automatically and tell your callers that everybody in your house is too busy to talk to them. And besides all these advantages, my easy-to-make personal home computer, which is the result of months of research, experimentation, and heavy drinking, can actually heat your home. Impossible, you say? Why not build it and find out?

First, head down to your home workshop and gather together the tools and materials you'll need.

MATERIALS

- Solder
- A television set

• 8 to 10 pounds of assorted electronic parts, which you can buy wherever electronic parts are sold. I find that transistors work best, although you can use diodes, provided they're fresh.

TOOLS

- A screwdriver
- An ice pick
- A drill
- A Bowie knife
- A hacksaw
- Something to melt solder with, such as a soldering gun or toaster

DIRECTIONS

Now you're all set. Remove the back from the television cabinet, and, using your ice pick, chip out the insides and throw them away. Next, using your Bowie knife, stab the top of the cabinet to create an eight-inch gash.

Now arrange your electronic parts on your workbench in an attractive display and melt solder on them until they all stick together, taking care not to drop too much molten solder on your dog. Next, you can either wait for the parts to cool off, or, if you're in a hurry, simply dump them in a bucket of water. (CAUTION: Never touch the hot parts with your bare hands. Ask a neighbor to do this.)

Once the soldered-together parts are cool, drill a few holes in them and screw them to the inside of your television set, using your optional hacksaw on either the television set or the parts to insure a good fit. Now all you need to do is reattach the cabinet back and check to make sure your fire insurance is paid up. You're ready to enter the World of Home Computing.

First, you'll need some data to put in, or "input." Have your children go around the house, inside and out, and gather up, or "up-gather," all your bills, check stubs, candy wrappers, receipts, lawn clippings, tax records, and lint balls. The more data you give your computer, the better it will work. To input your data, simply stuff it into the Bowie-knife gash.

Next, send your children to another room, or, if possible, another state; then plug your computer in. For a few seconds, nothing will happen, but then you'll hear the computer start to process, or "process," the data. Before long, you'll actually be able to see it working, even smell it; after 20 minutes or so, your computer will be processing data at such a rate that your entire house will be warm as toast. In fact, this easy-to-make personal home computer pro-duces heat so effectively that since I built mine, we haven't spent a nickel on home heating, primarily because of the medical bills.

Chapter 11

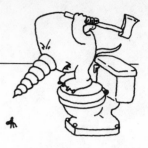

Household Pests

Getting tough with toads

In this chapter, we'll explore various techniques for reducing common household pests to lifeless blobs of tissue. Now before I get a lot of angry letters from ecology nuts, let me assure you that I am all in favor of wildlife, as long as it stays in its place, which is Africa. I believe that if God had wanted us to share our homes with insects, He would not have made them so unattractive.

Although the techniques described in this chapter are designed primarily for the smaller styles of pests, they will also work on larger ones, such as goats or people who want you to become an Amway distributor.

Termites

Termites are unattractive little insects that have developed a highly complex society, very much like American society, except that instead of houses they have nests, and instead of a president they have a queen. The queen

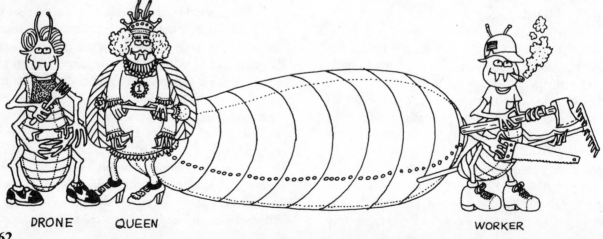

DRONE   QUEEN   WORKER

termite can lay up to 46,000 eggs a day, more than eight times the output of the most productive U.S. president, Grover Cleveland (1837–1908). So we can see that termites are indeed amazing creatures.

Beneath the queen in the termite hierarchy are the drones, and beneath them are the workers, who are chosen for their stupidity. Each day, thousands of workers scurry from the nest in search of wood, with the idea that they will chew it up and mix it with spit and bring it back to the queen. The queen doesn't want it, of course; nothing appeals to her less than chewed wood mixed with termite spit. So the instant they leave the nest, she and a few top aides swarm off to another house, probably yours.

The easiest way to keep termites away is to install a 6,000-volt, one-inch-high electrical fence around your house. This fence will keep out not only termites, but also most snakes. Of course, the snakes that do get past the fence are likely to be extremely angry, so it might be a good idea to wear a sidearm at all times.

Roaches

Roaches are the hardiest form of life on earth. In a recent experiment, scientists detonated a hydrogen bomb directly on top of a female roach, and the only noticeable effect

was that several days later she gave birth to 65,000 baby roaches, some of them weighing as much as three pounds.

Many people believe they can get rid of roaches by spraying them with poisonous chemicals, but this is utter nonsense. Roaches love poisonous chemicals. They'll often gather under the sink late at night and lick the residue off the Black Flag can. The more chemicals you spray, the more roaches you attract. This is how your professional exterminators stay in business.

The only surefire way to get rid of roaches is to remove all the liquor from your house. Roaches can mate only when they're drunk. Can you blame them? Would you mate with a roach if you were sober? So what roaches do is get really drunk, then have hurried, squalid sex amongst the filth and little rolled-up balls of grease and ketchup in the darkness under the refrigerator. The next morning the female lays 35 billion eggs and vows never to do anything so disgusting again, but by nightfall she and her mate are creeping up the side of the Jim Beam bottle again. Alcohol abuse is a terrible problem among roaches, which is why you see so few of them in positions of responsibility. So you'll be doing them a big favor if you get rid of your liquor. It might also be a nice idea if you and your family squatted in front of the refrigerator from time to time and had inspirational discussions about the evils of drink.

Children

You cannot simply spray toxic chemicals on children the way you can with roaches, because children represent our Hope for a Brighter Tomorrow. So the best way to deal with pesky children is to read them a few old-fashioned traditional fairy tales in which various deformed creatures ingest children who do not behave. At the end of the story, say: "See, Bobby? If you don't want the great big ogre with eyes that glow like red-hot coals in

PROBLEM: BLATANTLY OBNOXIOUS CHILDREN

NO-FAIL SOLUTION: WASH THEM (BUT EASY ON THE BLEACH)

the darkness to come into your room tonight and plunge his enormous yellow fanglike teeth repeatedly into your flesh, you must never set fire to Daddy's legs again." Or, if this approach doesn't work, you can simply place your children in the washing machine and set it on Spin Dry.

Mice

The best way to get rid of mice is to set traps. To illustrate why traps are so effective, let's look at what goes on behind the scenes in a mouse family.

It's a cold winter's evening, and Momma and Poppa Mouse are putting little Debbie and Jimmy Mouse to bed. "Oh, Momma," Debbie cries, sniffing her little pink nose as a tiny tear trickles from her deep, brown eyes to her soft, gray fur. "I'm so hungry I don't think I can sleep. Couldn't we have something to eat, please?"

"Now, now," sighs Momma Mouse. "You know how upset the humans get when we eat their food."

"That's right," chimes in Poppa Mouse. "And frankly, I don't want to upset the humans any more, because they've been acting mighty odd lately. The other day, they were squatting in front of the refrigerator and talking about liver damage."

"But Daddy," says little Jimmy Mouse. "If we don't get something to eat soon, we'll starve to death, and it's Christmas Eve. Besides, there's a stale old piece of cheese just outside the hole, and I'm sure the humans wouldn't mind if we ate it."

"You're right, Jimmy," says Poppa Mouse pensively. "I'll just go outside here and pick up this piece of . . ."

Toads

The only way I know of to get rid of toads is to clear the children out of the room and strike them (the toads) with hot pokers.

Chapter 12

The Lawn and Garden

Why all the plants in your garden hate you, and how to win their respect

You should take care of your yard, because it tells people a lot about you. For example, if you have a lot of yard statues, it tells people you're a jerk.

The most important part of your yard is the lawn. In America, having a nice lawn is considered a major cultural achievement, like owning a hardcover book or watching "Meet the Press." Americans would rather live next to a pervert heroin addict Communist pornographer than a person with an unkempt lawn.

Drugs and your lawn

The first step toward a nice lawn is to determine the chemical content of your soil. To

do this, dig up a handful of soil and examine it carefully under a harsh light: It should be composed of dirt, unless you live in New England, in which case it will be composed of enormous rocks; if you live in the South, your soil may also contain used tires.

Once you've determined the chemical content, you should add some random chemicals to your soil. Many lawn experts recommend that you add nitrogen, which is stupid, because nitrogen is a gas, and there is no way in the world you can add it to your lawn. It will simply drift off into the atmosphere the instant you open the bag. So your best bet is to just go up to the medicine cabinet and root around for some chemicals in the form of old prescription pills and dump them on your lawn.

I use old tranquilizers on my lawn, and not only have I saved a lot of money on chemicals, but I've also found that I have an extremely relaxed lawn. Take the earthworms. Instead of sliming around underground in a nervous, twitching manner, as so many worms do, my worms loll about on the lawn surface, laughing the laugh of the truly carefree. Oh, sure, sometimes they get underfoot, but it's a lot better than the time I gave them amphetamines and they were up all night shrieking about how nobody loved them.

Dandelions and crabgrass

Dandelions are easy to get rid of: You just jab them with red-hot knitting needles. Some people even eat them in soups and salads. Most of these people die within hours.

Crabgrass, the squat, ugly, tattooed plant that makes up 85 percent of your lawn, is tougher. Crabgrass can grow on bowling balls in airless rooms, and there is no known way to kill it that does not involve nuclear weapons. Oh, I know you've seen advertisements for lawn products that are supposed to kill crabgrass, but don't believe them. Crabgrass thrives on these products. In fact, my crabgrass often tries to dupe me into buying them. When I'm getting into my car, my crabgrass will yell, in mock horror, "Oh, please, don't go to the garden supply store and buy one of those deadly anticrabgrass lawn products!"

The only way to deal with crabgrass is to sneak up on it in the dead of night, pound it repeatedly with a ball-peen hammer, and flee on foot before it can snare you by the ankles. You won't kill the crabgrass, of course, but it may become irritated enough to move to a neighbor's lawn.

How to grow all of your food

Your first job is to prepare the soil. The best tool for this is your neighbor's motorized garden tiller. If your neighbor does not own a garden tiller, suggest that he buy one. Then select a section of your lawn or driveway that

looks as though it might have soil underneath it, and rip it up with the tiller. As the sharp steel blades slice violently into the ground, you may be able to hear the tiny screams of the various worms and furry little woodland creatures hibernating in the soil. Pay no attention.

Now you should buy some vegetable seeds, which are sold in little packets with attractive photographs on the covers to illustrate what your vegetables will not look like. The backs of the packets will give you specific planting instructions, depending on what area of the country you live in. For example, if you live in Florida, you should plant your seeds in the ground, whereas if you live in Maine, you should plant your seeds in Florida.

Once you have planted your garden, you have to deal with insects. The trick is to prevent them from eating all the seeds within minutes after you plant them, so they'll have something to eat later on. The best way to do this is to scatter sandwiches and pastries around the garden to distract the insects until the seeds have had a chance to form vegetables.

Larger animals, such as rabbits and elk, are tougher to keep away. You may have to fire a few bazooka rounds over their heads. This will also keep your neighbor at bay if he's trying to get his motorized garden tiller back.

Your only remaining task is to rotate your crops. About every two weeks, dig everything

up and put it where something else was. This may seem like a lot of work, but your major farmers do it all the time. For that matter, some of your major farmers manage to get out of growing crops altogether, and the government pays them for this valuable service. You might want to try setting up the same arrangement. Instead of starting a vegetable garden, write the government a letter like this:

"Dear Sirs: I didn't grow anything this year. Please send me $126,000."

I'd appreciate it if you'd let me know how the government responds, especially if it sends you money. If, on the other hand, armed federal agents arrive at your door, I'd prefer that you didn't mention my name.

Tips on Growing Popular Vegetables

Tomatoes

Tomatoes are the most popular garden vegetables, because you can do so much with them. For example, you can eat them. The trick to growing tomatoes successfully is to stagger the planting. Plant one-fourth of your tomatoes, then wait two weeks and plant another fourth, and so on, until you have planted them all. This insures that all your tomatoes will ripen within a five-minute period late in August, usually when you are away on vacation, so you will return home to find 700 pounds of tomatoes rotting on the ground in a sodden, insect-covered mass.

Zucchini

The zucchini is a dense, flavorless vegetable that is useful primarily as ballast. You can also eat zucchini, but only in very small quantities: One zucchini is enough to satisfy the zucchini needs of a family of six for a year. The trouble is, you cannot grow just one zucchini. Minutes after you plant a single seed, hundreds of zucchinis will barge out of the ground and sprawl around the garden, menacing the other vegetables. At night, you will be able to hear the ground quake as more and more zucchinis erupt. To prevent your property from becoming one big, pulsating zucchini herd, you will be forced to sneak over to your neighbors' houses in the dead of night and hurl excess zucchinis onto their lawns.

Cashews

Plant your cashew seeds about six inches apart, and be sure to salt them every four days.

Rhubarb

This hardy vegetable was a favorite of my mother's. Every year, she would produce an elaborate rhubarb pie, which was second only to Brussels sprouts in the category of things we kids would rather die than eat. Rhubarb is ideal for canning. You just put it in cans, stick the cans in your pantry, then move.

Corn

Your corn should be knee-high by the Fourth of July. If it isn't, you could be fined or jailed.

Chapter 13

Car Repair

The three keys to trouble-free motoring: animal traps, a wading pool, and this fact-crammed chapter

Most common car problems are caused by pets (see chart). The best way to avoid these problems is preventive maintenance, by which I mean always checking your car for pets before you start it. You should also change your oil all the time. This is what your top race car drivers recommend. Of course, your top race car drivers also routinely drive into walls at speeds upwards of 180 miles an hour, so I don't know that we should accept their opinions as gospel.

Handy car maintenance checklist

ENGINE. The engine is the large, filthy object under your hood, unless you live in a really bad neighborhood. To understand the importance of proper maintenance, let's take a look at what goes on inside your engine when you turn the ignition key. This will require you to cut the engine open with a blowtorch, but I

Handy Troubleshooting Chart		
Problem	**Cause**	**Solution**
Car emits foul odor when engine is running	Cat sleeping on engine	None
Car makes horrible noise when moving	Dog tied to rear bumper	Turn up radio
Car will not start	Something wrong with car	Change oil

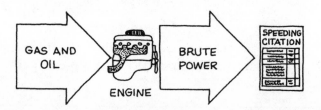

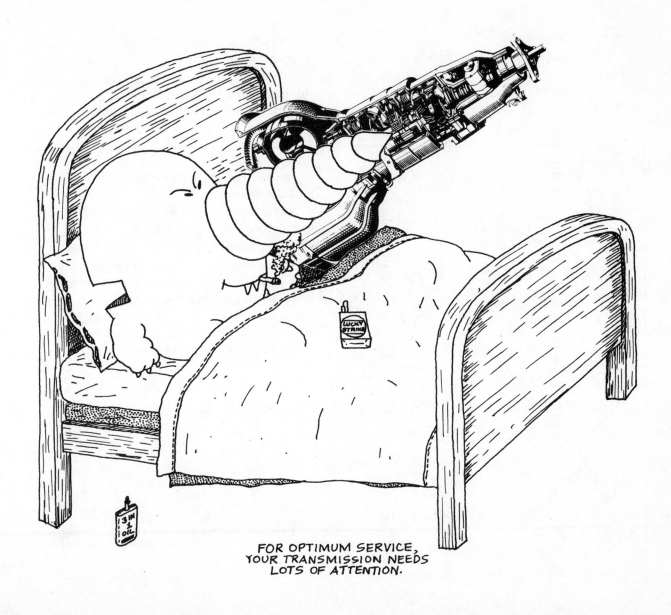

FOR OPTIMUM SERVICE,
YOUR TRANSMISSION NEEDS
LOTS OF ATTENTION.

think you'll be glad you did.

When you turn the key, gasoline comes rushing out of the gas tank and electricity comes rushing out of the battery, and they meet in the engine, where they explode with a force that could easily reduce the engine to hundreds of pieces of red-hot shrapnel traveling at high speeds and capable of destroying every living thing within 50 feet. But this will probably not occur if every one of the 63,000 parts that make

How to Change Your Oil

PROPER DRESS AND NECESSARY TOOLS

1. Start your car and allow it to warm up.
2. Lie on your back and inch along under the car until you locate a little boltlike object that you cannot remove without a wrench, then inch back out and locate a wrench.

3. Inch back under and rotate the boltlike object counterclockwise until oil starts gushing out, just like in those old movies where John Wayne and his sidekick discover oil and dance around, except whereas they are dancing vertically in glee, you will be dancing horizontally in pain, inasmuch as the oil has been heated to roughly 6,000 degrees by the engine.

up the engine is working perfectly, which is why you should maintain your engine. Every six or seven thousand meters, open up the hood and inspect the engine closely. It should have many random tubes and wires running off toward other areas of the car. Newer engines should also have oriental writing.

TRANSMISSION. The truth is, there is nothing you can do about your transmission.

4. Speaking of the engine, I forgot to tell you to turn it off. That should have been Step 2. I'll try to remember to correct that before this book goes to the printer, so as to avoid a lot of unnecessary engine damage and death.

5. Get some oil and pour it into an orifice in the engine until you see little rivulets of oil running across the driveway because you forgot to put the little bolt back in the engine, which I suppose I should have told you to do back in Step 3, which will be Step 4 once I move the current Step 4 to Step 2, where it belongs, but frankly, I'm tired of having to think of every tiny little detail for you.

Nobody knows how transmissions work, or even where they come from. They just arrive at car factories in unmarked crates, and the workers put them into the cars. Many people believe transmissions are created by beings from other solar systems. There is evidence to support this theory, namely transmission manuals, which contain bizarre diagrams and deranged alien commands such as: "Using a 6.57 reduction-ended canister wrench, rotate the debenture nut 6 degrees centigrade, taking care not to disenfranchise the gesticulation valve."

So if something goes wrong with your transmission, your best bet is to just give your car to the poor and claim a tax deduction.

TIRES. Tires are extremely important, for without them the tire industry, as we now know it, would cease to exist. You should inspect your tires frequently for signs of tread and obscure little letters and numbers on the sides, which represent significant events in the lives of the tire factory employees. For example, A78-13 means "All 78 of us tire factory employees went out and got really drunk last night, so maybe 13 of the tires we make today will be any good."

EXTERIOR. Your car's exterior takes a real beating, especially during the summer. Hour after hour, day after day, month after

month, the sun beats down on your car with harmful rays that can fade the paint and kill you if you spend any time outside trying to do anything about it. So the hell with the exterior.

EXHAUST SYSTEM. This is located under the car, smeared with road kills. From time to time you should hose it down or drive briskly through a wading pool.

Chapter 14

Redecorate Your House in a Day

And stick "aesthetics" back where it belongs, in the dictionary

The cheapest way to redecorate your home is to cover every horizontal surface in it with home decorating magazines filled with tasteful pictures of the interiors of homes belonging to people who spend more money on end tables in one month than you will spend on food in your entire life.

A much more expensive approach is to hire an interior decorator. Interior decorators are people who have spent years studying the principles of color, shape, and texture, until they have reached the point where they would rather die than agree with an ordinary person such as yourself on a matter of taste. So what you have to do is trick your interior decorator

into believing you want the *opposite* of what you really want. If you want a warm, cozy, intimate look, show the decorator a picture of a General Motors brake-assembly plant. If you want a rustic look, show the decorator a picture of the Sistine Chapel. You'll get what you want, and the decorator will think you didn't, so everybody will be happy.

Redecorating your kitchen in five easy-for-me-to-say steps

1. To get some inspiration, read a batch of home decorating magazine articles about people who completely remodeled their kitchens even though they're incompetent jerks. These articles always begin with a black-and-white photograph of a horrible, dingy, 1950s-

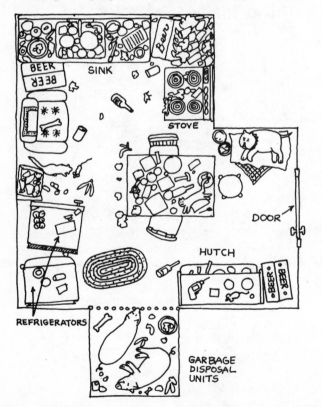

style kitchen, with unclean plates strewn all over and rats lounging around and waving at the camera. Then you see a glossy color photograph of a spectacularly modern kitchen that is clean enough for neurosurgery and is at least six times as large as the kitchen in the other photograph. It is obviously a completely different kitchen, probably in another state.

2. Once you have been inspired, take a hard look at your own kitchen. What don't you like about it? Is it the layer of grease and scum that has gradually built up on all the surfaces over the years, to the point where the insects have trouble getting enough traction to climb up to the counters? Or is it the color scheme? Are you among the millions of unfortunate American families whose appliances are Harvest Gold or (God help you) Avocado? Have you ever wondered why, of all the colors they had to choose from, major appliance manufacturers for many years insisted on making everything Harvest Gold or Avocado, two of the ugliest colors ever devised by the mind of man, colors more appropriate for stomach secretions than home decorating? Were they Dwight Eisenhower's favorite colors or something?

Whatever the reason, people finally came to their senses, and you can no longer find appliances in Harvest Gold or Avocado except in stores that have special sections catering to people with bad taste. Appliances now come in many attractive colors, all of which you should ignore, because appliances should be white. So should toilets. It is nature's way. It is the American way. I am sure that the only reason the U.S. Constitution does not specifically require that appliances and toilets be white is that the Founding Fathers never dreamed anybody would be stupid enough to use any other color.

3. Once you've decided on your color scheme (white), you should get a large sum of money somehow and go buy the actual appliances. The big issue here is whether you should get a regular oven or a microwave oven. A regular oven is hot inside, so when you put a tuna casserole inside, it gets hot. Is everybody with me so far? A microwave oven, on the other hand, is *not* hot inside. Instead, it has these tiny little rays (hundreds of them could easily fit into a woman's purse) that are manufactured in Japan. These rays travel *right through* the casserole dish at speeds approaching 250 miles an hour and slam into the tuna, causing it to get hot. The advantage of microwave ovens is that since only the contents get hot, you can pick the dish up with your bare hands. The disadvantage is that as soon as you open the lid, the microwaves come whizzing out in random directions, and could strike your eyeballs or furniture.

4. Once you've bought your appliances, you should get some graph paper and draw up a floor plan of your new kitchen, showing where

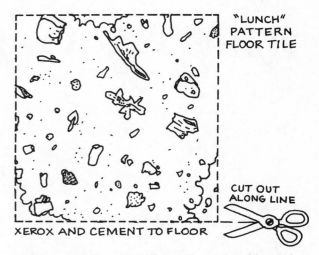

"LUNCH" PATTERN FLOOR TILE

CUT OUT ALONG LINE

XEROX AND CEMENT TO FLOOR

the new appliances will go. To make this project as difficult as possible, try to put each new appliance at least 11 feet from the one it's replacing. The only exception is the refrigerator. You must not move it, because all the jelly and ketchup you spilled under there over the years and never bothered to clean up has festered and evolved into a grotesque and durable life form that, if exposed to direct sunlight, could awaken and decide to take over the world. The responsible course is to put the new refrigerator on top of the old one.

5. Your new kitchen is almost done! All that remains is for you to take out the old appliances and put in the new ones according to your plan! And put in a new floor! And cabinets! And change the wiring and plumbing all around! Let me know how it goes.

Chapter 15

Build Your Own House

On second thought, don't

Here's a project for the really ambitious do-it-yourselfer with no grasp of reality: building an entire house. Not only will you save scads of money, but you'll be continuing a tradition that dates back to pioneer days, when our hardy forefathers used to whack down trees personally and form them into crude log cabins, which they would live in for maybe two days, after which they would migrate westward, because nothing in the world is worse than living in a crude log cabin. I mean, there's only one room, so you're all lying there at night listening to each other's bodily noises and smelling the aroma of congealing muskrat, or whatever pioneer dish you ate, and you hardly ever get any sleep. That's why everybody has such vacant stares in those old pioneer photographs.

So in the interest of continuing this fine old pioneer tradition, you should build your

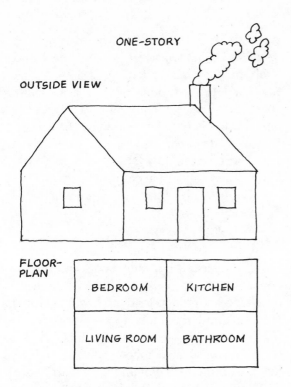

ONE-STORY

OUTSIDE VIEW

FLOOR-PLAN

BEDROOM	KITCHEN
LIVING ROOM	BATHROOM

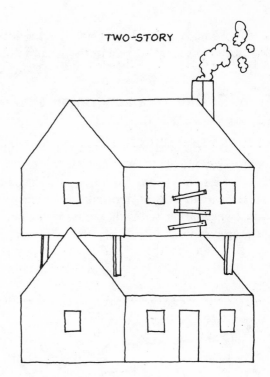

TWO-STORY

own house, following the easy, step-by-step series of steps below.

Step #1: Draw a plan

You should never start to build without some idea of what the house ought to look like when it's finished, so get yourself a piece of paper and a nice, sharp pencil, and draw yourself a house plan. The plan should consist of two parts: an outside view showing what the completed house would look like if it had smoke curling out of its chimney, and an inside view showing the location of windows, appliances, rooms, etc.

If you can't think of a house plan of your own, simply trace the one shown in the first illustration, which combines the advantages of elegant simplicity with the advantages of being very easy to trace. Feel free to modify the interior if you have any personal preferences, such as you'd like to have some way to get from one room to another. And if you think you'll need more space, consider the optional modular two-story house plan shown in the second illustration.

Step #2: Borrow an enormous sum of money from a bank

This is the trickiest part of home building, because you'll have to convince the banker that you know a lot about building, which is, of course, a lie. The best approach is to sprinkle your conversation with all kinds of technical building jargon.

BANKER: So, Mr. Jones, just how much money were you thinking of borrowing?

YOU (*showing your plan to the banker*): Well, as you can see from this plan, to insure that the lateral stability of the main structural cross-members is adequate for the stress on the head jamb likely to be created by the rotational torque of the upper sash top rail, I'll need to use a vapor degreasing system with at least 64 kilobytes of random access memory.

BANKER (*extremely impressed*): Here. Take $600,000.

Step #3: Get some land

Most local building codes require that houses be built on some kind of land. One excellent source of land is Iowa, which has scads of land that nobody ever uses for anything except growing corn, which is fed to pigs anyway, so I'm sure nobody would mind if you just took a smallish plot and built your house on it. The worst that could happen is that an Iowa farmer would tell you to move your house, and I doubt this would happen because every Iowan I've ever met has been extremely nice. Another advantage of Iowa is that it is located conveniently close to Kansas.

However, if you'd prefer not to locate your house in Iowa, don't despair, because there's lots of spare land around in other places, such as along the sides of interstate highways. Some of this land even has little picnic tables and people who come along from time to time to

mow the grass, so if I were you I'd snap it up before someone else does, or the Iowans start growing pig corn on it.

Another land source is estates belonging to the rich. Many of these estates are enormous, so the odds are the rich will never even notice you, especially if they are famous rock stars who travel most of the time and even when they're home they're not all that observant on account of they spend most of their leisure time trying on clothes and ingesting narcotic substances.

Step #4: Buy a large quantity of house parts

The main thing is studs. Studs are these boards that are sometimes called "two-by-fours" because they are not two anythings by four anythings (see Chapter 2, "Wood"). Most houses contain billions of them. You'll also need nails, a roof, and one toilet for each bathroom shown in your plan.

You can buy your house parts at a lumberyard, but as I pointed out back in Chapter 2 (see Chapter 2), the people who work in lumberyards are hostile and suspicious and they will probably try to trick you. You'll ask for studs, and they'll send you home with industrial sewage piping. So I recommend you get your house parts at a home center. The advantage of going to a home center is they give you little baskets and carts to put your house in, and you'll always know how much you're paying because there will be at least six price stickers on every stud. The only drawback is that most of the time the home center will be out of whatever you need, so you'll have to

make upwards of 600 trips (see Chapter 2 again; in fact, you might just as well stay in Chapter 2, for all the good this chapter is doing you).

Step #5: Standing on your land, attach the house parts together so they form a house shaped like the one in your plan

Building an entire house may look difficult, but all it really takes is a little common sense and a willingness to accept the fact that you will never finish no matter how long you live. At the beginning, when you're nailing large boards together, you'll think you'll be done in a matter of days, but pretty soon you'll realize that the only materials you have left are skillions of little pieces of molding and pipes and wires and doorknobs representing 600,000 man-hours of extremely tedious work, and you'll reach the point where all you do is sit on the floor and drink beer and fantasize that you live in a motel and you don't even have to fold your own towels. I know a couple who live in a semicomplete house that they once tried to build, and after a couple of years they stopped even noticing that they have a pile of lumber in their living room. They just dust it off and put cheese and crackers on it when company comes. So good luck! I admire your spunk. Really.

DON'T GET BOGGED DOWN WITH LITTLE DETAILS LIKE ERECTING WALLS.
YOU CAN SAVE HOURS AND DOLLARS BY INSTALLING THE WHOLE HOUSE
AT ONCE, RATHER THAN OVER A PERIOD OF DAYS OR EVEN WEEKS.

Index